THE RIVER NILE

In ancient times, the River Nile was much wider than it is today. It began in the lakes of equatorial Africa, passed through the highlands of Ethiopia and swirled its way northward along a huge fault in the earth's crust. Throughout its course, it plunged over six jagged cataracts, the last of which was 1200 kilometres from the sea. After the last cataract it began a slow meander to its delta. Here it branched out into several channels before flowing into the Mediterranean Sea.

In the sixth millennium BC, a steady process of desiccation was happening along the North African coast, creating desert from several formerly inhabited highlands. Inevitably the dispossessed people were driven towards the nearest and surest source of water — the Nile. The first settlers arrived *c.* 5000 BC. To begin with they made their homes inland, in the Nile valley: closer to the river lay marshland, sandbanks and flourishing papyrus beds, an area dominated by crocodiles and hippopotami. As the population grew, the land became divided in two: Upper Egypt (the Valley) and Lower Egypt (the Delta). Between them was an area of cultivable land encompassing about 20,000 kilometres.

The valley's climate produced abundant rainfall and the river and its tributaries provided a habitat for a great many animals and plants. The early people, whose society has become known as the Faysum culture, after the Faysum Lake, appear to have been keen fishers, hunters and cultivators of grain, such as wheat and barley — two of the staple foods in ancient Egypt. The Nile valley was the second area of the world, only Sumer was more advanced, where ancient peoples began to move away from a nomadic hunter-gatherer existence and develop communities.

The Nile was the lifeblood of the country. Each year, the Egyptians held a festival in her honour, extolling the annual floods which took place in late Summer and early Autumn. The floods provided water for the crops and coated the fields with rich silt, bringing new fertility to the land. The festival was a time of great feasting, a celebration of the land's re-birth and, in dynastic times, a tribute to the pharaoh. The Egyptian people believed their pharaoh to be a god and it was thought that his divine will controlled the rising river, the flooding of the land and therefore the prosperity of agriculture.

As well as providing life, the Nile was also the ancient Egyptians' coffin bearer. A fundamental part of the elaborate death ritual was the corpse's journey to its final resting place, when the mummy was carried across the Nile on a barge, symbolically beginning its passage to Osiris' portals. Replicas of these boats, fashioned from papyrus or wood, have been found in many tombs, representing the last earthly journey of the deceased. The river barge carried the coffin to the western bank of the Nile, from where it was taken to the edge of the Western desert, the traditional burial ground of the ancient Egyptians. The West was believed to be the land of the dead, as it was there that the sun went each evening to die.

Pharaoh of the 18th Dynasty (National Museum, Cairo). Courtesy of The Bridgeman Art Library. *(Overleaf and detail below.)* This gold image shows a pharaoh seated on his throne being attended by his queen. The royal couple are depicted beneath the powerful rays of the sun — a symbol of the blessing of the sun god, Re, stressing the importance of benevolent forces of nature in ancient Egypt. This artefact was found in the grave of Tutankhamen, a fairly minor pharaoh, but one who has assumed great prominence today due to the excavation of his tomb. Much of the knowledge we have about the ancient Egyptians comes from the objects discovered with his body.

· PHARAOHS & THEIR PEOPLE ·

Before 3100 BC, Egypt was not a unified land. It was divided into small principalities, or *nomes*: there were twenty-two *nomes* in Upper Egypt and twenty *nomes* in Lower Egypt. In time this became two distinct regions: the Valley (Upper Egypt) and the Delta (Lower Egypt). It was Menes, the first pharaoh (the word 'pharaoh' comes from Hebrew and means 'Great House'), who transformed the country into a unified kingdom. Between the reign of Menes and the last recorded pharaoh Nektanebo II, there were thirty-one dynasties of Egyptian rulers, spanning almost 3000 years. Within these three millennia, there were seven distinct eras: the Protodynastic era (3100–2700 BC), the Old Kingdom (2700–2200 BC), the First Intermediate period (2200–2052 BC), the Middle Kingdom (2052–1786 BC), the Second Intermediate period (1786–1575 BC), the New Kingdom (1575–1087 BC) and the Post-Empire era (1087–c. 342 BC). For ten years after the reign of the last pharaoh, Egypt was ruled by the conquering Persians until, in turn, they were vanquished by their long-term enemies, the Greeks, under the command of Alexander the Great. Alexander seized power in Egypt in 332 BC.

During the Protodynastic era (3100–2700 BC) the pharaoh became identified with the gods. According to tradition, he was viewed as the earthly incarnate son of Re, the sun god and one of the country's most popular immortals. The pharaoh was the father and mother of all his subjects, he had no equal and was worshipped as the specific deity of his people. By the 4th Dynasty, this had become a form of dictatorship. The pharaoh governed absolutely, with power over all aspects of his peoples' lives. The administration work was undertaken by *nomarchs*, bailiffs who travelled around the ancient *nomes* to resolve local problems and to collect one-fifth of the peasants' produce or money in taxes.

During the 5th Dynasty, Egypt became a turbulent place. The royal family began to divide and new tribes entered the country from Palestine and Syria, all wanting to establish their own communities and fighting over already settled land. There was resentment among the peasants over the crippling taxation system; the nobles and middle class sought power; *nomarchs* became the virtual rulers of their *nomes* — the country seemed on the verge of collapse. However, shortly before 2000 BC, the pharaohs of the 11th Dynasty managed to re-unite the Delta and Valley, and from this time onwards the country remained unified.

The 12th Dynasty marked the beginning of the Middle Kingdom (2052–1786 BC), a time of growing Egyptian military power. External trade, which had all but disappeared during the decades of strife, was resumed and strengthened. Egypt's fame and influence spread throughout the globe and her imperial era began.

The history of Egypt's rulers is a colourful one and enough to fill several books. It includes pharaohs such as Akhenaten, who strove to change the country's religious beliefs; Queen Hatshepsut who ruled as pharaoh thereby causing severe court etiquette problems by being female — it was finally decided to depict her wearing the royal heraldic beard; and the long-reigning, domineering Rameses II, reputedly the pharaoh of the Bible who is believed to have oppressed the Israelites.

In spite of a seeming wealth of archaeological evidence, there are still missing segments. We will never know the full story of the tombs which were plundered so long ago and many aspects of the lives of the pharaohs and their people may remain a mystery forever.

Death Mask of Tutankhamen **(National Museum, Cairo). Courtesy of AKG Photo London.** *(Overleaf and detail below.)*

The death mask of Tutankhamen is probably one of the best-known discoveries of ancient Egypt. The breathtakingly beautiful mask was created from gold and precious stones and even after centuries locked away in the bowels of the earth it is still untarnished. Tutankhamen's beard and headcloth *(nemes)* were the symbols of royalty in ancient Egypt — even Queen Hatshepsut had to be depicted with a regal beard. The cobra on Tutankhamen's forehead was believed to protect the pharaoh by spitting poison at his enemies.

· THE FIRST PYRAMID ·

The best-known and most enduring image of Egypt has to be of the majestic pyramids. The pharaohs of the Nile erected pyramids as grand mausoleums, monuments befitting deified rulers. These tombs were composed of many chambers, each with a specific purpose, and the building and decorating of the houses of the dead called for great skill in architecture and craftsmanship.

The first pyramid to have been built is the earliest large stone structure still remaining on the earth today, and is probably the first such monument ever constructed (c. 2680 BC). It was designed by one of the greatest architects ancient Egypt ever produced, Imhotep. Ironically, his name has retained a greater reputation than the pharaoh, Djoser (also known as Neterikhet), who commissioned the pyramid. While Djoser has slipped into relative obscurity, Imhotep has gained immortality. He became the object of religious veneration and, 2000 years after his death, was still worshipped as a god of wisdom.

Djoser was the first great ruler of the 3rd Dynasty and Imhotep was both his Chancellor and the High Priest of the sun god Re. Djoser's 62-metre-high pyramid was built at Saqqara, the necropolis ('city of the dead') of the capital city, Memphis. It was created from a core of desert stones and finished — after Imhotep had altered the plans five times during the building process — with polished limestone; the first use of limestone on such a scale. The limestone was carved in steps to ensure that after death the pharaoh could climb up the side of his pyramid to ascend to his father, Re.

Beneath the pyramid was an underground burial chamber, surrounded by lavish passageways, decorated with relief sculpture. The corridor walls were inlaid with blue-green ceramic tiles designed to produce the appearance of a screen of reeds. Set amongst these are depictions of Djoser performing the jubilee ritual. The ritual was a reconfirmation of royal authority in Egypt and the pharaoh is shown running around markers representing Egypt's boundaries.

The magnificent tomb was set within a sumptuous courtyard, surrounded by stone columns and subsidiary buildings; these included a mortuary temple to ensure that the people could continue to worship Djoser after his death. The construction of the pyramid must have taken thousands of men many years to complete. Contrary to popular belief, these labourers were not slaves. Compared to most imperial powers the ancient Egyptians have relatively few periods of human bondage in their history, although their peasants were treated little better than serfs. The artisans who built Djoser's tomb would have been his employees, labourers who believed that by performing such work their ruler would provide for them in the afterlife. Many of these men probably realized their ambition sooner than expected: over 10,000 burial urns were found in Djoser's tomb, probably containing the remains of the servants it was considered he would need in the next world.

This scene dates from the 18th Dynasty, it was discovered in the tomb of Nebanoum. The delicate painting illustrates the diversity of plant and animal life provided by the Nile: a large number of bird species are featured, along with fish and butterflies. A man (presumably Nebanoum) and a cat are depicted hunting together, both have caught three birds and the man grasps an asp in his left hand. The two women in the background are harvesting flax. The colourful hieroglyphics tell of the life of the dead man.

· THE GLORIES OF GIZA ·

Egypt has over eighty pyramids, all of which are located along the West Bank of the Nile. Of these, the most famous were built at Giza: three magnificent stone edifices dedicated to the pharaohs Khufu (or Cheops), Khafra and Menkaura.

Giza lies a few miles north of Saqqara (close to modern Cairo), and the pyramids here date to within 75 years of the death of Djoser (c. 2680 BC). They are powerful representations of the Old Kingdom, built with money gained from taxing the people and erected for the glory of their rulers.

The first, and largest, of these wonderful mausoleums was built for Khufu, a pharaoh of the 4th Dynasty, c. 2600 BC. The tomb was constructed of almost 6,000,000 tonnes of stone (each of the limestone blocks weighed nearly 16 tonnes) and it reached a height of 146 metres. When built it would have been visible for miles in every direction. It is a masterpiece of technical expertise: the rock base is astoundingly even, varying no more than a centimetre at any point; and the orientation of the pyramid is almost perfectly aligned with the points of the compass. Contained within the catacombs are a tomb chamber and a chapel connected by passageways, all beautifully constructed in a manner befitting a pharaoh.

In front of Khufu's great memorial are three small pyramids; these contain the bodies of his wife and children, with one exception. Khufu's son Khafra was the pharaoh for whom the next great pyramid was built. It stands close to that of his father and in perfect alignment with the Sphinx: the pyramid in the West and the statue in the East. The Sphinx at Giza is only one of several sphinxes erected throughout Egypt, but it is the most famous of them all. It is usually thought to represent the head of a woman and the body of a lion, as immortalized by the Greek playwright Sophocles (c. 496–406 BC) who describes it in *Oedipus* as the 'dog-faced witch'. More recent evidence, however, suggests that the head is actually that of Khafra, possibly from a sculpture left over after the building of his tomb. Some sources claim that Khafra saw the Sphinx thereby proving that the image could not be his, though as his tomb would have been built before his death, the argument is tenuous. Either way, the Sphinx was the protector of all the pyramids at Giza and was also believed possessed of magical powers. When one stands before the Sphinx looking up at that amazing face, the overwhelming impression is of wisdom and antiquity. This incredible sculpture has stood for over four thousand years, suffering only a pugilist's nose from the passage of time.

The remaining pyramid was erected for Menkaura, Khafra's son, who ruled after the death of his father. He appears to have been a popular, just, studious and mild ruler. His coffin is now in the British Museum in London and the mummy case bears the following inscription:

Osiris, King of the North and South, Menkaura, living for ever, the heavens have produced thee.... O King of the North and South, Menkaura, living forever.

Around the perimeter of the pyramids lie various less-salubrious tombs, these contain the bodies of the pharaohs' officials and advisors. The effectiveness of a royal tomb, and therefore the welfare of the dead pharaoh's people, depended on the rituals performed by the mortuary priests. Even after the death of a ruler, the people's reverence continued, strong in the belief that he would watch over them and ensure their protection in the next world.

Two Upstanding Statues of the 18th Dynasty **(National Museum, Cairo). Courtesy of AKG Photo London.** *(Overleaf and detail below.)* These figures were found in an 18th-Dynasty grave, they date from **c.** 1340 BC. Statues such as these were common tomb adornments and the burial chambers of the pharaohs Khufu, Khafra and Menkaura would have contained similar figurines, representative either of the pharaohs and their families or as servants to provide for their master in the next world. These particular sculptures are of a man and woman, presumably the deceased and his wife. The man's lower body and legs are covered with gold-painted hieroglyphics.

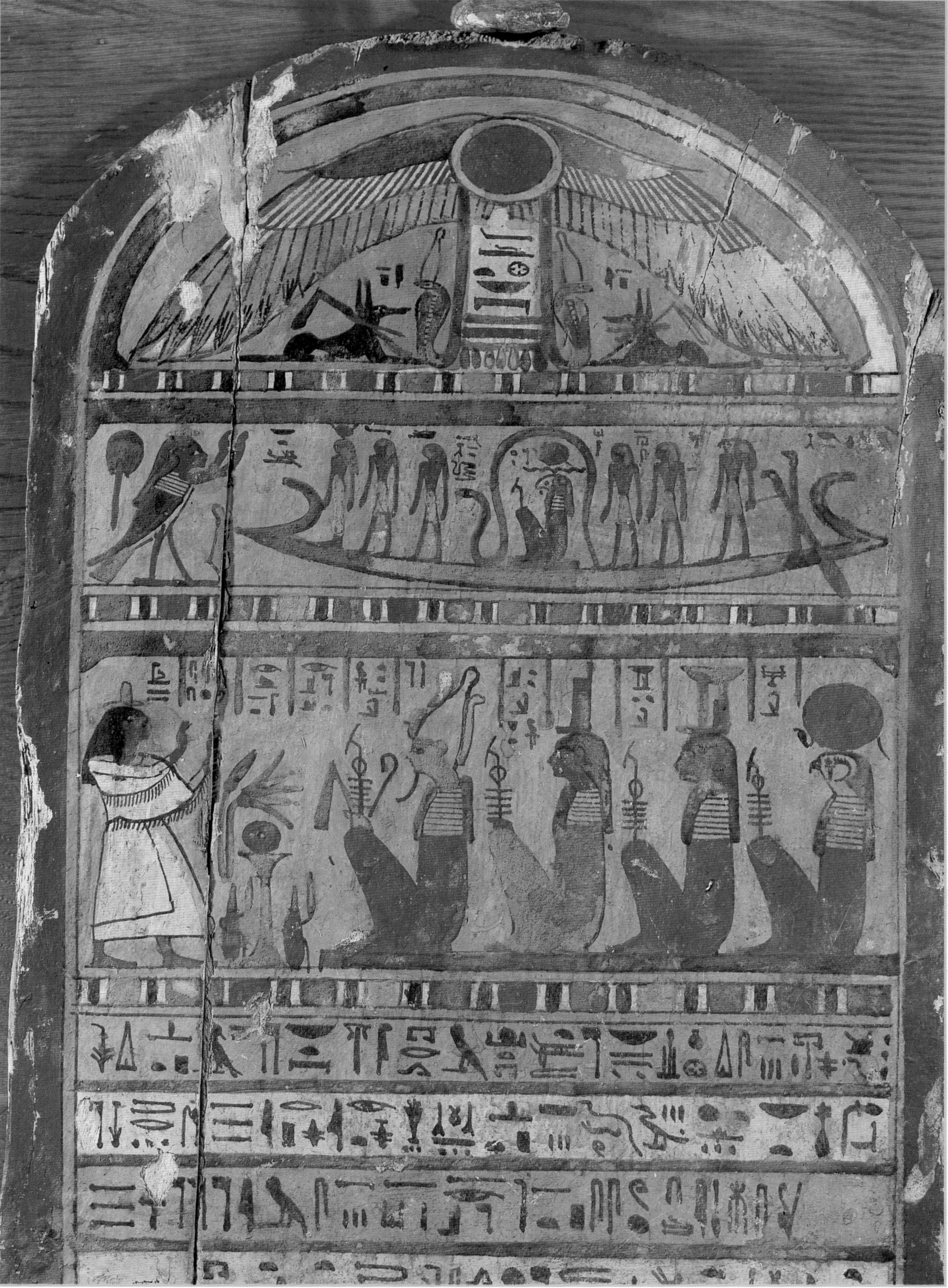

· HIEROGLYPHICS ·

The word 'hieroglyphics' comes from the Greek: 'hieros' meaning 'sacred' and 'gluphos' meaning 'carved signs'. Although the concept of writing may have originated in the East, the symbols used were definitely Egyptian in origin. The ancient Egyptians developed their unique style of writing into an art form which puzzled academics for centuries. Until the work of European scholars in the 18th and 19th centuries, it appeared that the pharaohs' people had taken the key of their hieroglyphics with them to their graves.

Hieroglyphics are found wherever a scribe was required to mark an event, be they engraved on stone or wood, or written on papyrus. The direction of the writing varied from object to object, seemingly determined by the surface it was inscribed on rather than by a pre-set pattern. Whether recording praises to the pharaoh, verses of literature or religious eulogies, these fascinating symbols were inscribed in mesmerizing rows on the walls of both tombs and temples. The execution of the writing is painstakingly skilful, and the individual symbols are beautiful works of art in themselves. The language is composed of a unique combination of phonetics and ideogrammatics and the variety of signs is legion. There are emblems for specific sounds, syllables and even single consonants; for instance the name Rameses is composed of three symbols which translate to RA MS SS.

Scribes were employed in all aspects of everyday life and hieroglyphics became absorbed into the culture. They produced two new distinct forms of writing: cuneiform, a less pictorial system which used wedge-shaped characters; and hieratic script, a shorthand version of hieroglyphics. The oldest known papyrus texts (dated to *c.* 2500 BC) are administration documents written in hieratic script.

With the waning of Egypt's power, and the increasing importance of Greek and Latin in Egyptian administration, the use and understanding of hieroglyphics also declined. By the 4th Century AD, they were neither used nor understood. For centuries the carved symbols endured as a powerfully mysterious reminder of a long-gone civilization. The secrets of the Sphinxes, the Pyramids and all the treasures within seemed destined to remain an enigma.

It was not until AD 1789, with the arrival of Napoleon Bonaparte, that Egypt's long-forgotten language began to come back to life. Bonaparte set sail to invade Egypt for two reasons: partly to open up a new trade route to India (the French had been ousted from their original route by the British), but also on a voyage of discovery. As well as taking a large number of soldiers, Napoleon also recruited an army of scholars. He took botanists, geologists, mathematicians, astrologers, chemists, draughtsmen and cartographers. His ambition was to unlock the secrets of the pharaohs and to chart an as yet unmapped country.

At first Napoleon's quest was unsuccessful on both counts, but in 1799, a French soldier made a remarkable discovery. While digging the foundations for a fort at Raschid, on a branch of the Nile near Rosetta, he unearthed a lump of carved black stone. This piece of basalt was the single most important find in hieroglyphic research; it has become known as the Rosetta Stone.

Funerary Stele in Wood (Archaeological Museum, Florence). Courtesy of e.t. archive. (Overleaf and detail below and above.)
This exquisite wood carving features several rows of hieroglyphics. Together with the pictures, the hieroglyphics relate a journey to the Underworld. The top picture shows the encompassing power of the sun god. Below that is a voyage along the Nile, the sky god Horus is seated in the boat flanked by attendants and protected by a snake. Beneath is the Underworld, realm of Osiris, the father of Horus. Osiris is greeting a row of souls, at the front of which is the spirit of a pharaoh, indicated by his royal beard.

· THE ROSETTA STONE ·

The Rosetta Stone was recognized instantly as a monumental breakthrough. Plaster casts and written copies were made of the carvings and hurriedly sent back to France. Egyptologists throughout Europe renewed the quest for understanding. A breathtaking new era in Egyptology was dawning.

The reason for such fevered excitement was a wonderful new perspective offered by the Rosetta Stone and the realization that this could be the long-awaited key to the deciphering of hieroglyphics. Hieroglyphics were carved in the top section of the stone, however this in itself was unexceptional — they were no different from those elsewhere in Egypt and were therefore equally indecipherable. Beneath the familiar symbols, however, were two further sections of writing: the middle section was in Demotic, the last-known version of ancient Egyptian writing and, most importantly, a language of which the world still retained some knowledge, thanks to the few words which remained as part of the Coptic language. Crucially, however, the lowest section of the stone was inscribed in ancient Greek — still the language of thousands of scholars throughout the western world. Here, at last, was the key to the puzzle.

One of the first hurdles to be overcome was a misconception which had begun soon after the understanding of hieroglyphics was lost. Throughout the Arabic-speaking world it had been claimed that every symbol encapsulated an entire word or magical meaning. The Rosetta Stone's two comparative pieces of text were to show whether, or not, this belief was true.

It was a painful process and one which took twenty-three years to reach fruition, but the deciphering of hieroglyphics was eventually cracked through the painstaking work of two men: a Frenchman, Jean François Champollion, a professor in Egyptology at the Grenoble Academy, and an English physician and mathematician, Thomas Young.

Young, an accomplished linguist, began his research after finding a transcript of the Rosetta text. His scientific abilities helped him to an understanding of the mathematical hieroglyphics, while his knowledge of well over a dozen languages enabled him to begin a comparative study of the three very different linguistic elements used on the stone. Although he is seldom credited for his work — Young eventually sent all his discoveries to Champollion who kept very quiet about the debt he owed Young — the secrets of the ancient Egyptians might never have been uncovered had it not been for the exhaustive work of such a brilliant mind. For example, it was Young who made the discovery that the *cartouches* (rectangular loops encircling certain groups of letters) denoted the name of a king.

However, in spite of Young's discoveries, the true master of hieroglyphic discovery is undoubtedly Champollion. The Frenchman spent half of his short life (he died suddenly at the age of 42) working on the Rosetta Stone's text. It is a life's work of enduring wonder and has bequeathed a legacy of information that has carried the study of ancient Egyptian life and culture into areas that were once considered impossible.

Decorated Fragment of Gold Sheet. Courtesy of Christie's Images. (Overleaf and detail below.)

This fragment of gold relief was found in the tomb of Tutankhamen. It depicts the pharaoh flanked by the falcon-headed Horus (to the right) and Osiris. In the top left-hand corner of the main section are two *cartouches* — groups of hieroglyphics encircled by a 'rope-loop'. The script from the Rosetta Stone enabled an Englishman, Thomas Young, to make the discovery that *cartouches* denoted the name of a king. He handed over his work to a Frenchman, Jean François Champollion, who continued the painstaking labour of unravelling the mystery of hieroglyphics.

EGYPTIAN ART & ARTEFACTS

The art of dynastic Egypt had little to do with individual creativity or expression. The painting, sculpture and architecture of the Nile's land was produced either in honour of the pharaoh or for the good of the state and continued to follow the artistic codes specified during the Protodynastic era (3100–2700 BC), which held true for almost 3000 years.

Nature and her gifts: the flooding of the Nile, the growth of the crops, the daily round of the sun, and the alternating seasons, were popular subjects for artistic representation; as were people, depicted in both statues and portraits. Art in all its forms was a means of extending life, a way to capture the essence of a person or natural force to ensure that they would last for eternity.

Sculpture was created from clay, bone, ivory, stone and wood and, very rarely, from metal. It appears to have been an important art, found particularly in tombs in the form of imposing statues of the deceased and subtly carved pictorial reliefs. Many of these relief scenes illustrate the life of the dead person.

Egyptian sculpture tended to be very stylized, with few personal characteristics to differentiate the chosen subject from any other; for instance the death mask of Tutankhamen is relatively indistinguishable from facial depictions of other pharaohs. This is likely to be because artists followed a decreed pattern: every pharaoh had to be depicted with the royal beard and wearing the royal headcloth (*nemes*). The *nemes* was usually encircled by a cobra, the symbol of the pharaoh's protection against his enemies. These rigid rules of portraiture allowed little leeway for idiosyncrasies. However, during the Middle Kingdom (2052–1786 BC) an interesting change took place: the portrait heads of pharaohs became lined to show care for their subjects and a concern for justice.

Strangely, the human body is always depicted rigidly, in both sculpture and paintings. Despite a well-developed knowledge of anatomy — something that is apparent from the mummification rituals and from the discovery of written and illustrated documentation of surgical practices — limbs are set in an unwavering stylized fashion and the torso shows little, if any, capability of movement. People and gods were often portrayed in the three-quarter profile style that is a familiar characteristic of Egyptian art.

An area in which the ancient Egyptians excelled was the decorative arts. They left a rich legacy of beautifully painted pottery, delicate jewellery, elaborate clothing and carefully worked metals. Popular decorations included lotus and papyrus flowers and buds; tendrils of grapevines; fruits such as pomegranates and figs; humans and sacred animals. Pottery seems to have been used both for utilitarian purposes and for its purely ornamental value: painted lamps, bowls, and tiles have been found in abundance showing varying degrees of usage.

Jewellery was fashioned from precious gems, translucent stones, horn, shells and bones, with adornments for the hair, neck and arms seeming particularly popular. Although little clothing remains, from studying the paintings of different dynastic eras, one can see the intricacy of the design and follow the change in fashions.

The beauty of Egyptian metalwork is perhaps nowhere more evident than in the fashioning of weapons. Daggers, scimitars and short swords were made from silver, gold, bronze and copper, with handles of ivory, bone and horn. Many of the weapons contain intricate patterns created from delicate wires of gold and copper or sections inlaid with precious stones.

The Mummy Mask of Yuya (Egyptian Museum, Cairo). Courtesy of e.t. archive. *(Overleaf and detail below.)* This exquisite piece of gold sculpture dates from the New Kingdom (1575–1087 BC). It is the death mask of Yuya, Master of the Pharaoh's Horse. Yuya and his wife Thuya were not of royal blood, but their daughter married Amenhotep III and gave birth to a son, the religious reformer Akhenaten. This beautiful artwork is made from gold, coloured glass and semi-precious stones. Breaking with the tradition of stylized art, the skilful artist has created a true portrait, with realistic ears and eyes and an almost imperceptible smile upon the lips.

· LIVING FROM THE LAND ·

Egypt's early settlers were drawn to the banks of the Nile because of the agricultural quality of the land. By the time the pharaohs rose to prominence, their people had created a self-sufficient, cultivated landscape. From the humble beginnings of individual farmers eking out a living, Egypt eventually became one of the greatest agricultural exporters of the ancient world.

In early times, Egyptians lived in tiny villages. Their homes were of mudbricks — Nile mud mixed with wheat chaff, a further indication of the peoples' dependence on their river — and were carefully sited away from any cultivable land. The great river was able to provide everything the people needed: the farmers dug canals to divert the water and irrigate their fields; and the banks and currents provided edible wildlife with lush plants, ducks, eels and fish in abundance. Aside from the benefits provided for the land and food, the river was also a means of communication and transport. In such a favourable landscape the life of an Egyptian farmer was a fairly secure one.

By the dynastic era, much of the land was owned by a few wealthy men who leased their land to farmers; several legal documents have been discovered concerning this. A lease started at the beginning of the ploughing season and ran for one calendar year. Typical payment for the land seems to have been one-quarter of the farmer's harvested crop, thus he would not be bound to pay an impossible amount of money to the landowner if the harvest failed.

Egypt had three distinct seasons: Inundation, when the Nile flooded its banks (late Summer and early Autumn); Going Down of the Inundation, when the crops were planted; and Drought, when the grain crops were harvested (March and April). The farmers grew emmer wheat and barley. These were important staples of the Egyptian diet, used to make a variety of foods from bread to beer. Flax was also harvested as were grapes and other fruits. Trees were bled for precious saps, and reeds were used to make papyrus and household equipment, such as sieves for grain harvesting. Pairs of wooden winnowing fans were also used for the grain harvest: the grain was thrown into the air while the fans created a breeze to separate the chaff from the wheat.

As well as the crops, Egyptians kept animals, to eat and for agricultural and sacrificial purposes. Pairs of oxen were used to plough the fields as well as for beef. In a similar way to modern battery farming, animals were force-fed and kept in small stalls to ensure they were fat enough to provide a worthwhile feast or a magnificent sacrifice. A few years ago, archaeologists uncovered a now-famous depiction of a prize bull, fattened to such an extent that his legs could no longer support his weight. From the 18th Dynasty onwards it appears that cattle began to be branded to show ownership: bronze branding irons dated to that time have been discovered.

A variety of agricultural implements, such as hoes, sickles and mattocks have been found. In general, these have wooden handles and blades of bronze or flint. Another interesting archaeological find is leather containers which appear to be grain measurers. Grain was an important part of the bartering system and measures such as these would have been a vital part of a trader's equipment.

Scarab Pectoral Found in the Valley of the Kings at Thebes, (Egyptian National Museum, Cairo). Courtesy of Giraudon/The Bridgeman Art Library. (Overleaf and detail below.) The scarab beetle was regarded as divine and played a hugely important part in the life of ancient Egypt. The tiny black dung beetle was invaluable to farmers as the presence of its colonies provided a richly composted soil, essential for the growth of healthy crops. Scarabs are often depicted in works of art; in paintings and especially in jewellery. Scarab rings were particularly popular as were pectoral pins, such as this one made from gold and precious stones.

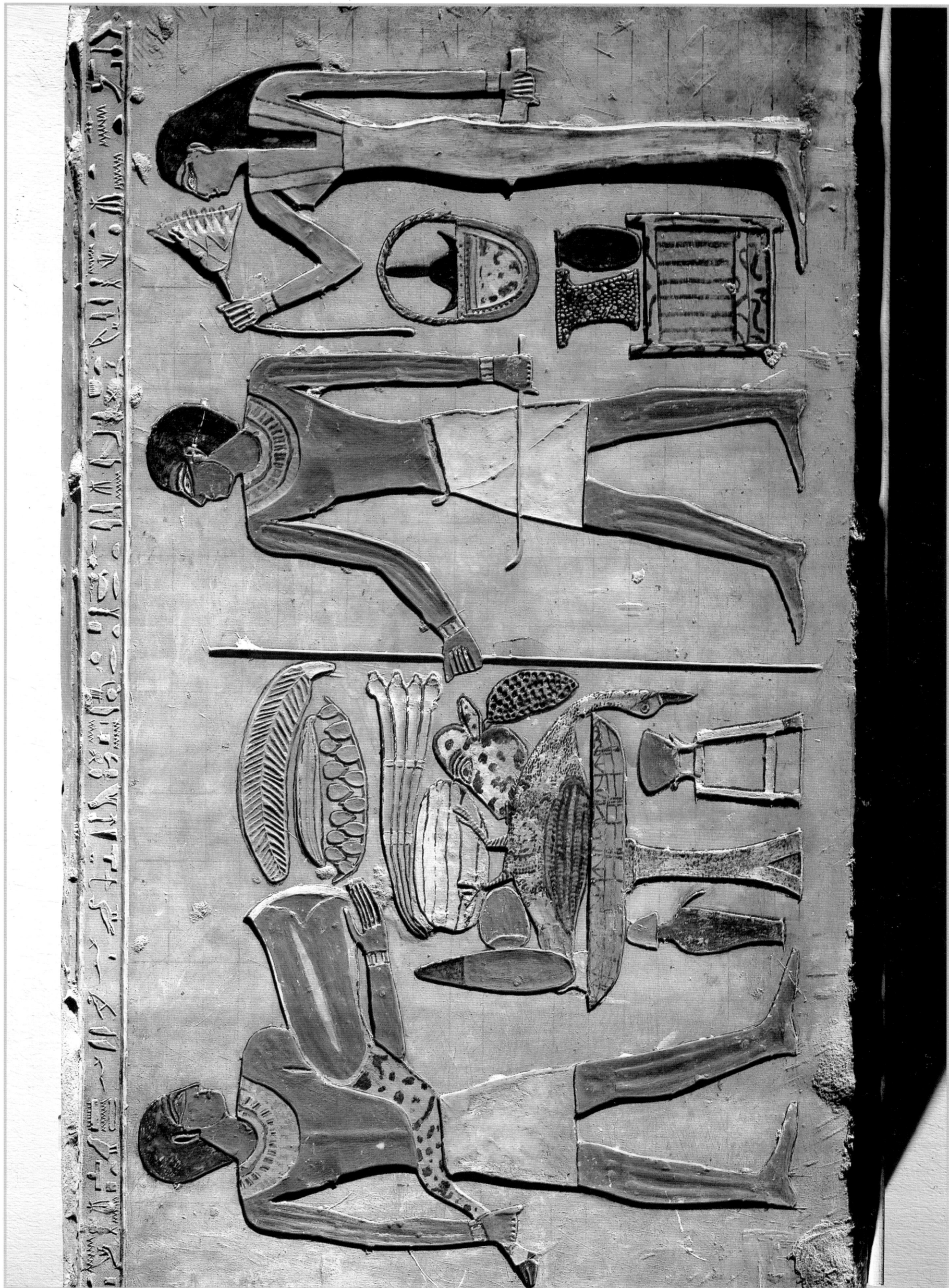

· FOOD & DRINK ·

Before Egypt began trading with other areas of the ancient world, her people had to be self-sufficient. The farmers grew grains and vegetables, they reared animals and birds for consumption and sacrifice to the gods, they fished in the waters of the Nile, made wines and beer and grew succulent fruits such as dates, grapes, figs and pomegranates. As products of the Nile and the sun, as sustainers of life and providers of intoxication, food and drink were seen as gifts from the gods and were frequently used as wages or as part of the barter system. Surplus food was stored at temples to guard against starvation in times of plague or drought. It is said that the temple of Osiris at Abydos could hold enough grain to feed 20,000 people for a year.

Eating was a celebratory and sociable affair, food was cooked over charcoal fires with beef, duck and other fowl the favourite meats of the wealthy. Fish was also enjoyed throughout Egypt: once caught it was immediately gutted, salted and laid out to dry in the sun.

Pomegranates were one of the most popular fruits. They were eaten widely and feature in many illustrations or as now-mummified funerary offerings found in tombs and temples. A famed aphrodisiac of the time was created by mixing crushed pomegranates with rose water and, although the actual recipe is unknown, pomegranates are the assumed ingredient of a widely consumed — and very intoxicating — drink called *shedeh*.

The most common alcoholic beverage in ancient Egypt was beer. It was made from barley and fermented bread, for which reason beer and bread were usually made together. Egyptian beer was not particularly potent and had a very short shelf-life — in large households it was made freshly every day. Beer was drunk throughout the year and given free as a gift from the pharaoh on feast days. Drunkenness was not frowned upon as it was seen as a means of bridging the gap between the living and the dead.

Figs, grapes and dates were also very popular. They were eaten as fruit, baked in cakes and

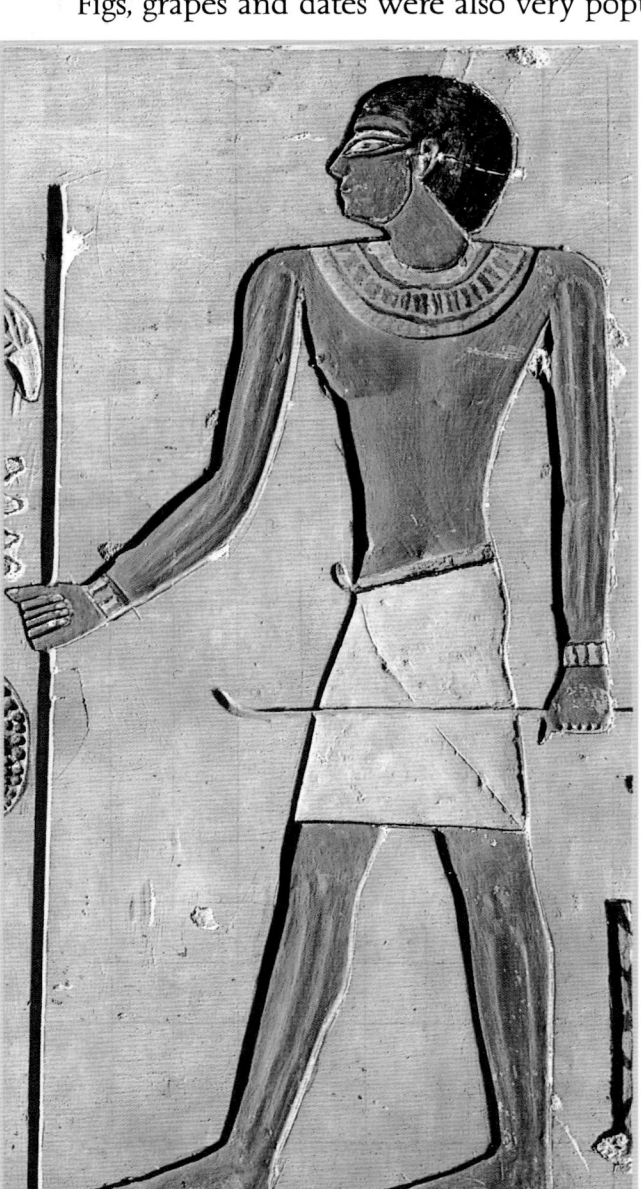

biscuits and used for making a variety of wines. Fig wine is little known, but traces of it have been found by archaeologists, and palm wine, as well as being a popular intoxicating drink, was used chiefly in the art of embalming. Another important palm tree is the Dom Palm, a native tree of Upper Egypt. The flesh of its fruit was used in cakes and the hard kernel (commonly known as 'vegetable ivory') was used for carving small ornaments.

Wine made from grapes was never as common or as popular as beer, and was probably used mainly by wealthy people on special occasions. All wine jars had to be stamped with the vintage and vineyard of origin, and from this archaeologists know that a vineyard on the western river in the Delta was probably one of the largest. Certainly more wine jars and labels have survived from this vineyard than any other. There were also vineyards in the Oasis of El-Kharga in the western desert of the Nile valley.

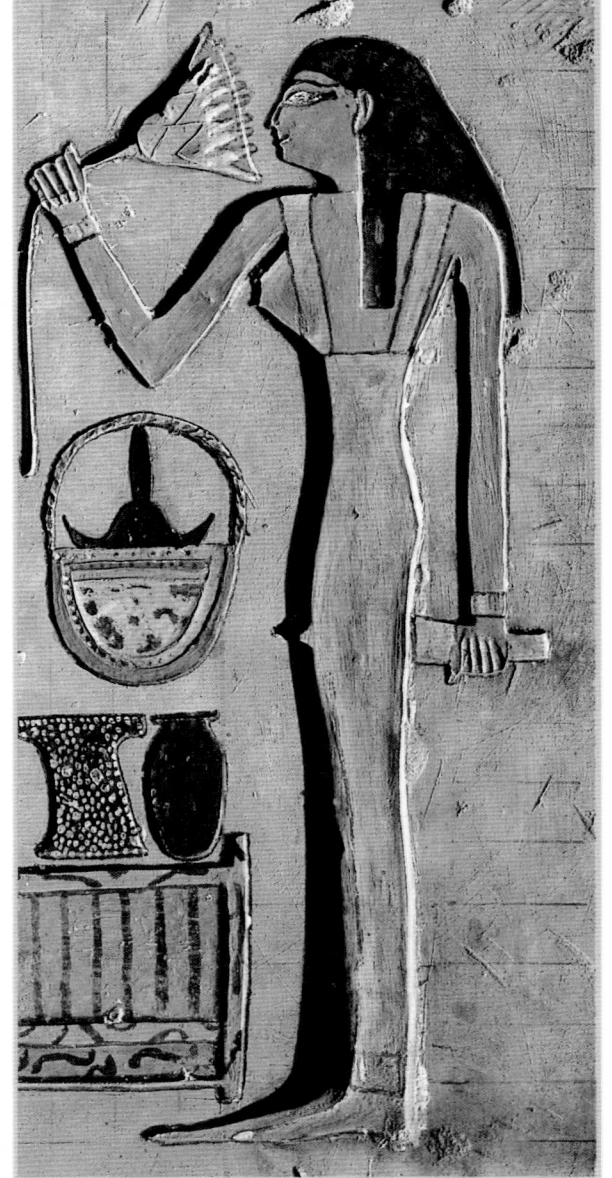

Relief of Cheti c. 1980 BC **(Akadamie der Bildenden Kunste, Vienna). Courtesy of AKG Photo London.** *(Overleaf and detail below.)*

This Middle Kingdom (2052–1786 BC) stone carving shows a table laden high with funerary offerings. Among the items which can be recognized, are a dead bird, onions, bread and a jar of beer (on the floor). The man at the right side of the relief is holding the entire back leg of an animal, hoof included, the animal's head can be seen on the table. Typical funerary offerings included meats, bread, cakes, onions, cucumbers, fruits (dates, figs, pomegranates and the fruit of the *nabk* tree) and beer.

· CREATION OF AN EMPIRE ·

In the early years of dynastic Egypt, there was little call for empire building. The first pharaohs had their work cut out keeping the ancient *nomes* of Egypt united, without attempting to gain new territories.

From the 1st Dynasty onwards, import and export trade was established, as were royal expeditions to seek new resources. Explorers were sent to the mines of Sinai; to travel upriver in search of spices, ivory and incense and downriver for the much-coveted Cedar of Lebanon; voyagers set out to bring back new species of animals; but this was exploration, not warmongering and was accepted if carried out in the spirit of peace.

However, at the end of the Middle Kingdom (2052–1786 BC), the pharaohs' sovereignty began to disintegrate. Military incursions by the rulers of Palestine added to the problems and eventually the pharaohs were overthrown. The Egyptians named these new kings 'Hyksos' ('rulers from a foreign country'). For a century, Egypt chafed at the bit beneath her new monarchs. The Hyksos introduced several new ideas: horse-drawn chariots, spoked wheels, archery, advanced weapons and new-style forts. Their reluctant subjects took notice, and under the guidance of a new pharaoh, Ahmose I, threw off the yoke of the Hyksos, forced them out of Egypt and pursued them into Palestine. This conquering hero was the founder of both the 18th Dynasty and the age of Egypt's Empire. Either as a result of a century of dented pride or a sudden desire to prove the strength of their country, Egypt became an imperial power for the first time.

Imperialism reigned triumphant. Pharaohs and generals led their victorious forces under the divine protection of Amen. They wrote swaggering accounts of their glorious deeds: records of victories were inscribed on temple walls and onto large stone tablets erected for the purpose. The accounts of battles are numerous, although it is unknown whether the inscriptions are accurate or owe more to inflated military pomposity.

The effects of Empire were manifold: foreign produce was now readily available in Thebes; foreign prisoners of war and slaves walked through the streets in all manner of dress and exhibiting alien customs; even more strangely, women of foreign royal houses became the Queens of pharaohs. Previously pharaohs seldom married out of their family, choosing to marry their sisters or daughters to keep the royal line pure, but now they were marrying outside their race.

This golden age remained vibrant until *c.* 1353 BC, when Amenhotep IV ascended the throne. Concerned about the rising importance of priests and the threat this posed to the pharaoh's divinity, he began a time of religious reform. His mission was to rid Egypt of polytheism, insisting that there was only one god, Aten, to be worshipped through the pharaoh. Amenhotep changed his name to Akhenaten (which means 'Effective for Aten') and founded a new capital city, Akhetaten, midway between Thebes and Memphis. Throughout his reign, the religion of Aten was practised and his divinity was unchallenged. When he died, *c.* 1335 BC, the old religions returned and Thebes was reinstated as the capital city.

Too concerned with internal affairs to notice what was happening elsewhere, Akhenaten and his religious reforms brought the Empire under threat of attack. After his death, Egypt's power continued to wane and the future of the once glorious Empire seemed dangerously uncertain. Aid appeared in the shape of Rameses II, also known as Rameses the Great, who came to power in *c.* 1297 BC. His reign lasted for sixty-seven years during which time he humbled Egypt's old enemies Syria and Palestine and fought the Hittite Empire. Throughout his reign, Rameses erected many temples, dedicated to himself and the gods; fathered over one hundred children and left Egypt an enduring legacy of its greatest ever pharaoh.

Gold Relief Depicting Ostrich Hunting (Egyptian Museum, Cairo). Courtesy of AKG Photo London. (Overleaf and detail below.) Modes of Egyptian transport changed little until the end of the Middle Kingdom (2052–1786 BC). The conquering Hyksos, and the ensuing age of Empire, provided the ancient Egyptians with many new inventions. The invading Palestinians drove much lighter, quicker chariots than those previously seen along the banks of the Nile. They also introduced the art of archery to their new subjects, as is demonstrated in this hunting scene. Later Egyptian skirmishes with the Hittites also brought about a new era in chariot building.

· DEATH & MUMMIFICATION ·

The earliest known Egyptian graves predate the dynastic eras and were little more than shallow pits. The curled-up body was often wrapped in the skins of animals or bound in reed matting. Sometimes the body was placed in a wooden coffin. The coffins were not elongated, as coffins are today, but were of a shape to contain the contracted, foetal-position corpse. At a later date tombs were covered with burial mounds — the precursors of the pyramid.

By the end of the Old Kingdom (2700—2200 BC), tombs were being equipped with a variety of models connected with the pastimes of the deceased. These were to ensure that the dead person enjoyed as good a standard of living as in the life he or she had departed. Replica houses, fashioned from pottery or wood, were also placed in tombs as a substitute home for the soul. These were often perfect models of the home the deceased had left behind: including gardens with pools and storehouses replete with food and drink. Typical funerary offerings included beer, meats (especially duck and beef), bread, cakes, onions, cucumbers, fruits such as dates, figs, pomegranates and the fruit of the *nabk* tree.

However, these elaborations seem of little consequence when compared to the opulence of the tombs belonging to the pharaohs. The most complete example of such splendour is the tomb of the young Tutankhamen. Throughout the world, people have marvelled at the treasures excavated from his grave: the wonderful gold and lapis lazuli death mask, golden chariots, life-size statues and an incredible abundance of gems and precious metals, 3000-year-old clothes and his spectacular mummy case. Even more startling is the realization that Tutankhamen was actually a very minor pharaoh who ruled for only nine years. Just imagine if the grave of Rameses II, whose reign encompassed 67 years, had been found intact. One can only speculate at the untold treasures contained within the catacombs of his tomb.

Before being placed in the tomb, a corpse was mummified ('mummy' comes from the Arabic for 'pitch-preserved body'). At first this was a ritual reserved solely for pharaohs, but from *c.* 2300 BC it appears to have been available to anyone who could pay for it.

At the start of the process, all internal organs (except the heart) were removed and placed in four *canopic* jars, the stoppers of which were fashioned into the shape of either the dead person's head or those of the gods. The heart remained in the body as it was believed to control thought and action, both needed in the afterlife. The body was then washed with spiced palm wine, covered in natron (a drying, antiseptic salt) and left. When the drying process was complete, the body had its original shape restored by being packed with linen and spices. The corpse was then coated with resin for waterproofing, wrapped in linen and placed in its case. The mummy case was used to shield the body from grave robbers and to provide a home for the spirit. Sometimes several mummy cases were used, placed one inside the other.

It was believed that the souls of the dead journeyed on to the next world in the company of Anubis, the jackal-headed god of death. Belief in Anubis appears to have been present since documentation began, but during the Old Kingdom (2700—2200 BC), a second god associated with death became popular. He was Osiris, the ruler of the Underworld.

The Egyptians' seeming preoccupation with death may appear macabre, but in fact, it stemmed from a fervent love of life and a profound religious belief in its continuation in the next world.

Tomb of Tutankhamen. **Courtesy of AKG Photo London.**
(Overleaf and detail below.)
This scene from the tomb of Tutankhamen illustrates many of the ancient Egyptians' beliefs about death and the afterlife. At the right-hand side of the wall paintings is a picture of the god of death, Anubis. Typically Anubis is depicted with the head of a jackal; in one hand he holds an ankh — the T-shaped cross with a loop at the top which was the symbol of eternal life. A painting on the wall above the dead pharaoh's head depicts a funeral barge on the River Nile.

· GODS & RELIGION ·

One of the most important aspects of life for the people of the Nile was their religion. The ancient Egyptians had many gods, worshipped in a variety of different forms, and their religious beliefs shaped all other aspects of life.

Before the unification of the land, each *nome* had its own sacred totem, worshipped in the form of an animal, be it a sacred cow, eel or toad. These deities were defended bitterly in territorial battles.

A higher order than these local gods was that of the greater gods, worshipped in animal and human form. These were believed to have been created by the divine forces which had also created the world.

Among those gods, the sun god, Re, was worshipped as the provider of heat and light ensuring growth of the crops. His god-fearing people were wary of offending him and celebrated his rebirth every morning. The East was believed to be god's land, whereas the West was the land of the dead. Each evening the setting sun was watched with anxiety and with prayers that he would rise again the next day. Re was also believed to be the father of the pharaohs and, from the 4th Dynasty onwards, he grew steadily in popularity, personified as a powerful combination of nature's forces.

Two of the most important gods of ancient Egypt were Osiris and his son Horus. According to legend, Osiris was a good king who was murdered by his evil brother Seth: Osiris is often identified with the life-giving forces of agriculture and Seth with the life-destroying desert. After his murder, Isis (Osiris' widow) resuscitated him temporarily in order that he might father her child. After which Osiris passed to his new kingdom — the Underworld. There he received the dead and passed judgement on their earthly behaviour.

Isis named her son Horus. When he grew up he slew his father's killer and became a great god in his own right. He is usually depicted as a falcon and worshipped as the sky.

Of all the animals that are held sacred, the most revered was the cat. One of the most powerful of all Egyptian gods was the dual personality cat goddess, known as both Bastet and Sekhmet. She represented the twin forces of good and evil: Bastet bestowed life; Sekhmet destroyed it. Sekhmet was believed to be responsible for plagues. Countless effigies of the cat goddess were made and worshipped. The killing of a cat was murder and punishable by death. The Greek writer, Herodotus, who wrote about his travels through Egypt c. 450 BC, stated that if a domestic cat died of a natural death, the family all shaved off their eyebrows in mourning.

Cats became big business. They were mummified and worshipped in their own temples; the temples had specially assigned priests who appear to have set up a lucrative trade in cat mummies. X-rays have revealed that many of the so-called cat mummies actually contain the bones of dogs, birds and frogs — obviously there were not enough dead cats available to supply the demand.

Perhaps it is because most of our knowledge of Ancient Egypt comes from the temples of its gods and the tombs of those who worshipped them that this ancient land still exerts such a potent fascination.

Stele of Ofenmut **(Metropolitan Museum of Art, New York). Courtesy of Visual Arts Library.** *(Overleaf and detail below.)*

This stele was found in the tomb of Ofenmut. The picture is of Ofenmut making an offering to Horus, god of the sky, who is often depicted (as here) with the head of a falcon. Horus was the son of Osiris, god of the Underworld, and Isis, Osiris's sister and wife. After the murder of Osiris, Isis brought him back to life in order that he might father their son. Horus and Osiris were two of the most important gods in the ancient Egyptians' world.

SELECT BIBLIOGRAPHY

Breasted, J. H., *Ancient Records of Egypt*, Russell (New York), 1962; Brugsch-Bey, Heinrich (trans. M. Brodrick), *Egypt Under The Pharaohs*, John Murray (London), 1902; Dodson, Aidan, *Monarchs of the Nile*, Rubicon Press, (London), 1995; Gombrich, E. H., *The Story of Art*, The Phaidon Press Ltd (London), 1957; Hobson, Christine, *The World of the Pharaohs*, Thames and Hudson, London, 1987; James, E. O., *The Ancient Gods*, Putnam (New York), 1960; Newland, S. L., *Rameses II*, CAXTON EDITIONS (London), 1997; Rohl, David M., *A Test of Time*, Random Century (London), 1996; Starr, Chester G., *A History of the Ancient World*, Oxford University Press (Oxford), 1983; Wilson, John A., *Culture of Ancient Egypt*, University of Chicago (Chicago), 1956; Winlock, H. E., *Rise and Fall of the Middle Kingdom in Thebes*, Macmillan (New York), 1947

For Mark and Sarah

First published in Great Britain by CAXTON EDITIONS an imprint of The Caxton Book Company, 16 Connaught Street, Marble Arch, London W2 2AF
Copyright © 1997 CAXTON EDITIONS

ISBN 1 84067 000 2
A copy of the C.I.P. data is available from the British Library upon request.

Created and produced by Flame Tree Publishing, a part of The Foundry Creative Media Company Limited, The Long House, Antrobus Road, Chiswick, London W4 5HY

Grateful thanks to Helen Courtney.